Fishing for Leads

Change Your Bait, Sharpen Your Hooks, and Reel in New Business!

RICK HILL

iUniverse, Inc.
Bloomington

Fishing for Leads
Change Your Bait, Sharpen Your Hooks, and Reel in New Business!

Copyright © 1993, 2012 by Rick Hill.
Some portions of this book are reprinted from a September 2004 edition of *The Fishing Trip and Don't Trip into the Podium* by the same author.

First Edition, April 1993
Second Edition, September 2004
Third Edition, January 2012

Cover design and illustration by Jerry "Skid" Rockwell

This book is written for educational purposes only.

All rights reserved. No part of this book may be used or reproduced by any means, graphic, electronic, or mechanical, including photocopying, recording, taping or by any information storage retrieval system without the written permission of the publisher except in the case of brief quotations embodied in critical articles and reviews.

iUniverse books may be ordered through booksellers or by contacting:

iUniverse
1663 Liberty Drive
Bloomington, IN 47403
www.iuniverse.com
1-800-Authors (1-800-288-4677)

Because of the dynamic nature of the Internet, any web addresses or links contained in this book may have changed since publication and may no longer be valid. The views expressed in this work are solely those of the author and do not necessarily reflect the views of the publisher, and the publisher hereby disclaims any responsibility for them.

Any people depicted in stock imagery provided by Thinkstock are models, and such images are being used for illustrative purposes only.
Certain stock imagery © Thinkstock.

ISBN: 978-1-4759-1498-6 (sc)
ISBN: 978-1-4759-1500-6 (hc)
ISBN: 978-1-4759-1499-3 (ebk)

Printed in the United States of America

iUniverse rev. date: 04/21/2012

This book is dedicated to the following:

Earl Nightingale, speaker and founder of Nightingale/Conant: In 1968 and ten thousand feet up in the air, I listened to a *Lead the Field* cassette tape series that told me how to be the Man on the White Horse instead of the Boy on the Black Mutt.

Bill Gove, first president of the National Speakers Association: Bill gave me hundreds of thousands of dollars of coaching for free—just because I made him laugh.

Gary D Burke, Shaklee Lifetime Master Coordinator: He never really taught me anything, but he *showed* me how to do a lot of things.

Contents

Acknowledgments ix

Don't Let Your Babies Grow Up to Be Salespeople

My Introduction to Sales 1
My First Sales Job: White Almond Bark 3
My Second Sales Job: Blonde Hair, Blue Eyes, and a Training Bra 6
My Third Sales Job: Apricot Kernels and Coffee Enemas 8
My Fourth Sales Job: Soaps and Pills 10

Are You Fishing or Cutting Bait?

Studmuffin Learns a Lesson 13
Death by Dancing 15
Let's Define a Couple of Terms 18
Drift Fishing, or How I Blew Lunch 19
Cracker Jack and Uncle Sam 21

Seven Fishing Techniques

Find Five Good Fishing Holes 25
Pop Quiz #1 28

Change Your Bait 31
Sharpen Your Hook Develop a One-Sentence Commercial 33
Pop Quiz #2 38
Fishing With Purpose Your Mission Statement 40
Finding Hungry Fish 45
Pop Quiz #3 50
Fishing with Nets 52
    Things Had Changed 53
    The Importance of Public Speaking 54
    My Format for Speech Writing 56
    Move #1: The Takedown Introductions That Claim
    Attention 57
    S I L E N C E 63
    The Proposition 63
    The Transitional Sentence 64
    Move #2: The Switch 65
    Sample Propositional Outline 65
    Move #3: The Pin Hold Closes That Leave the Crowd
    Wanting More 66
Pop Quiz #4 71
Weigh Your Catch The Qualification Process 73
    Using The Internet and Social Media to Fish with Nets ... 76
    Fire Hosing on Facebook and Twitter 82
    Make it Easy to Buy from You 84
Pop Quiz #5 86
Porky and Daffy Graduate 88

Acknowledgments

Hindsight is always 20/20 and a wonderful tool when one is sixty-one years old and rewriting his business books. The best advice I have at this stage of life is this: as early as you can, find successful people in your chosen field who are having fun and copy like crazy. My father, Wild Bill Hill, was next in line to be the president of Dodge before he slugged his boss. Still, I saw in him some characteristics to copy, not the least of which was wearing shiny shoes and driving a clean car. He certainly had his share of fun.

Ken Gordon discovered the first Mail Boxes Etc. store near San Diego while traveling and became the first franchisee with the second store. Today, Ken has over three hundred The UPS Stores in his area franchisee group, and his franchise skills are legendary. I heard Ken say over and over, "If it ain't fun, I don't want to do it." Suffice it to say, I learned a lot about franchises from Ken, but I learned a lot more about having fun.

Some of the MLM giants at Shaklee that I got to copy included Bob Holker, Bob Giddens, and Gary Burke. I copied personalities like Ron Fink of The RGF Environmental Group and Joe Boccuti of Tyent USA who focused on fun and were both brilliant in developing new business. Dr. Brent Allen, DO, not only knows a lot about integrative medicine but also has a sharp eye for business and helped me a lot when I fell from my white horse.

I tried to copy people who were having fun while they were making money. The people who were making money but not seemingly having much fun? Not so much.

Thanks to my brother Roger, who edited at least two editions of this book. And last but not least, thanks to Lisa Sasevich, who really did teach this old dog some new tricks.

INTRODUCTION

Don't Let Your Babies Grow Up to Be Salespeople

My Introduction to Sales

The studio became suddenly quiet on the set of the game show *Password*. The teams were tied, and time was running out for the defending champion. Small beads of perspiration dotted his upper lip as he glanced repeatedly at the small card in his hand—the card that held the secret password. The home audience heard the announcer say in hushed tones, "The password is *salesperson*."

Nervously the champion began.

"Uh, sleazy!" he blurted.

"Drug dealers!" his partner shouted with only seconds left in the game. The clues continued.

"Uh, uh, obnoxious . . . slimy . . . uh, pushy!

The contestant suddenly blurted the answer. "Salesperson!"

"That's it!" the host screamed. "You've won a brand-new car!"

The crowd went wild. The defending champion won a new Chevette and a year's supply of York Peppermint Patties. And we, who make our living as commissioned salespeople, were not at all entertained by the public's image of salespeople.

To parody the country western song: "Mamas, don't let your babies grow up to be salespeople. Let 'em be doctors and lawyers and such."

Those of us who select sales as a career may have an image problem. I started selling when I was thirteen years old. I didn't learn to sell correctly until I was twenty-four. But I thought I could sell when I was thirteen. Maybe you do too.

I've been a straight commission salesperson for more than thirty years now. And after personally selling and managing sales groups, most people who love to sell usually hate to prospect. Most would say, "Bring us qualified leads and we'll close 'em."

But finding new people to do business with has been, and always will be, the single most important aspect of the sales game. This book is designed to do one basic thing for you: teach you how to develop a never-ending chain of new business. It's a book about the art and science of prospecting.

To be able to move to a new community and in ninety days have all the business you need is a powerful skill. To walk into a room full of people you have never met and walk out with several qualified leads is peace of mind for straight commission salespeople.

My First Sales Job: White Almond Bark

My sales career started with selling boxes of white chocolate almond bark in the seventh grade. I sold more white bark than any other kid. My first year, I won a transistor pocket radio. Imagine. I sold over $500 of this candy and won a $25 radio. That's a 5 percent commission—and for door-to-door sales? Around Detroit? Next year things would be different. Things had to be different because I'd met the woman of my dreams. She was witty, beautiful, and the only girl I knew in the seventh grade who was developing. But she was from Warren, Michigan, where everyone lived in little brick cookie-cutter houses with carefully sodded lawns and built-in pools. They were the forerunners of today's yuppies. And Cheryl's mom wanted her budding pup to find another yup. I was a greaser (like the Fonz) who lived in a house with no lawn to speak of, and the only pool in our neighborhood was in the street after a heavy rain.

Next year I'd make a bundle of money and ask Cheryl to go steady. Her mom already said she didn't want her daughter running with people from "that" part of town. Maybe if I had a ton of cash?

The next year was 1963. Roseville, Michigan, was a blue-collar suburb of Detroit and had a lot of fund-raisers for education. Most of the families were lower middle class and worked in the stamping plants of the Big Three automakers.

I signed up again for the candy sale. But this time, my friend Larry Luba and I decided to steal 250 boxes, sell them, and keep the money. *Wait till Cheryl's mom sees all this cash!* I thought.

School let out that day about three o'clock. At precisely 3:03 p.m., I was on the front doorstep of my first prospect. We had stolen the candy earlier in the day and hid some of it in the AV room and some in our lockers.

"Good afternoon, ma'am. My name is Rick," I chirped. "I'm with the local school lunch program. Since my family can't afford the school lunches for me, if I sell just a few of these boxes a day . . ."

It worked like magic. In less than a week most of the candy had been sold, and lots of parents were feeling really good about helping that little guy with the sad eyes and curly hair get lunch every day.

It was all a lie. Sort of. It was true that we couldn't afford school lunches, so I delivered milk to the classrooms on milk break and set up chairs in the lunchroom for a free hot lunch every day. But come on, who wants to do that?

One day the vice principal, Mr. Reeser, got a phone tip that told him who had stolen the candy. Larry claims to this day that he didn't tell a soul, but then we both may have been bragging just a little.

Reeser "the Greaser" found me in the AV room munching on some white almond bark. It didn't impress him at all that I had masterminded the single largest white bark heist in the history of education. It didn't even impress him that my closing ratio was way above 95 percent. He didn't even care that I had practiced my pitch on my little sister, who was also keeping the books. He grabbed me by my Brylcreemed do and dragged me down the hall to the principal's office and expelled me. Worse yet, I had to return the money *before* I could show Cheryl's mom my bankroll. He made me return one dollar for every box stolen, over 250 boxes!

I didn't mind. I'd sold it for two dollars a box.

My Second Sales Job: Blonde Hair, Blue Eyes, and a Training Bra

It was now time for the second sale of my career: Cheryl, my childhood sweetheart, and her mom.

Cheryl and I met at church camp. Often Gratiot Avenue Baptist Church would take their young people to the local YMCA to swim. This was my chance to show her the depth of my love and see her ever-changing shape in a swimsuit. I waited for her to emerge into the pool area from the girl's locker room and quickly climbed the steps to the diving board. I called down to her, "Hey, Scscscher-r-r-yl (at that time I slurred my *S* sounds, and I stuttered)." I jumped toward her and shouted, "I l-l-ove you!"

But I misjudged the distance to the edge of the pool by just a few inches. I only remember her looking adoringly on as my chin hit the edge of the pool. Out cold. Sank like a rock. Tough sale.

Things didn't go so well with her mom either. By the time we were seniors in high school, her mom began hiding when I'd come over. When I confronted her mother with the possibility that her daughter and I might get married someday, her daughter told me after leaving her house that her mother screamed and stuck her head in the oven. An electric oven. Alas, her mom succeeded and we never got married.

So I didn't make the sale. No one makes every sale. No one.

We flunk our way to the top.

My Third Sales Job: Apricot Kernels and Coffee Enemas

College slipped by, and I moved to New Ulm, Minnesota, to work in a parochial school. I married a girl I had met in college, and things were going okay until I got terminal cancer after one year of marriage. Boy, can she pick 'em! I was twenty-three years old (for a complete account of this, in case you or someone you know has cancer, visit our website at http://www.freespeakersgroup.com and order a copy of *The Cancer Conundrum*).

The Mayo Clinic got first crack at me with about eight hours of surgery and a prognosis of embryonal-cell carcinoma, stage III. Chemotherapy after surgery was regarded as mandatory. Then I asked for a referral. Being a sales type, I figured I was about to spend tens of thousands of dollars on some drugs that would instantly make me a Hair Club for Men customer. I asked the chemotherapist for a couple of leads, people who had used chemo and benefited from it. No names. Not one. I figured the only way I was going to talk with these former patients was in prayer. So one night, I pulled out all my connections like Hemovacs and IVs and conducted a marketing survey. I interviewed some of those currently undergoing chemotherapy and asked them if they would recommend the program. None.

That same day I received a letter in the mail from a friend who suggested I consider the results some people were having from using vitamins, diet, and Laetrile in Mexico.

I called him for some leads. Six. Six names. I called these patients, and they said, "Run, don't walk, out of the Mayo Clinic and head for Mexico." I did. On the basis of a solid sales technique, I grabbed my hat and spent three weeks at the Oasis of Hope (www.oasisofhope.com) clinic learning how to eat raw squishy things, swallow tons of vitamins, take coffee enemas (without cream and sugar), and read ingredient labels to find out if nitrates were hidden in Jell-O.

This led me into my next sales job.

My Fourth Sales Job: Soaps and Pills

My next sales job was, you guessed it, vitamins—vitamins and other products from an MLM (multilevel marketing company). Ever been to a sales meeting for a multilevel company where they draw circles on a whiteboard illustrating how quickly your income can grow? Now I began selling pills by drawing circles on a whiteboard. Tough sale.

The first seven months were a disaster. Working full-time for seven full months, my income at Shaklee was barely over $200. Things began to heat up at home.

Understand that I thought I was ready. I'd listened to Earl Nightingale's *Lead the Field* series, my goals were written down and laminated in plastic, and every day I wrote out my to-do list in the order of importance. I was motivated, organized, and disciplined.

And broke. Earl hadn't covered this.

One morning changed my life. It could change yours. It was the single most important lesson of my business life. Read on.

PART I
Are You Fishing or Cutting Bait?

Studmuffin Learns a Lesson

I was up early as usual, ran a couple of miles, and, after having showered and shaved, came enthusiastically downstairs in order to breakfast *lightly* on organic toast and fruit. I started looking at the morning paper when my wife of two years said to me, "Studmuffin, I want to talk to you, and I want you to listen to me." We had two small children and a very small income.

I could see the muscles in her jaw tighten, and I knew this was not the time to scan today's late-breaking headlines. Basically, my future ex-wife said this: "No one is going to knock on the door of our apartment and ask us for an order. Not now, not ever. We have got to learn how to go find people. Now!"

I knew that. See, I was doing something for seven months that you've probably never done. I was getting ready—really getting organized, learning all I could about the product line and the company. I was reading motivational books, listening to cassettes, and organizing my office. Rubber bands never touched paper clips in my desk drawer, my inventory was symmetrically placed on the shelves, and my Rolodex was typed. I did everything . . . but talk to people. How come?

Because sometimes people say no.

I hate "no." I've heard sales trainers on DVDs say, "I love 'No!' Go for the 'No!'" These people would lie about anything. They must gargle with gravel.

Death by Dancing

Some say that when you sneeze, you come closer to dying than any other time in your life because your heart stops beating momentarily. This is not true.

The closest that a man ever comes to dying, in this life, is when he asks someone to dance and she says no.

Ever ask a lady to dance who said no? One night a long time ago, a buddy of mine and I were out at a local watering hole. As the evening wore on, I noticed a couple of lovely ladies standing on the edge of the dance floor, moving to the music and, it seemed to me, had signs on their foreheads that read, "Ask us to dance." I decided my buddy Bob should walk across the floor and ask them to dance. I'm a good friend to let him go first, huh?

When he was halfway there I noticed that every guy in the place was watching him like a cow on the slaughterhouse ramp. Someone had done this earlier. Everyone could hear his every step as he neared the end of his life. He was the lone Christian facing the lions. A hush fell over the crowd.

"Hi," he said. "Want to dance?"

There are times in our lives when all of life's meaning is focused on one event. This was such a time. She turned, looked at his face and, I think, his rear, and said, "I don't think so, no."

His life passed before his eyes. He gave her the Elmer Fudd laugh, and as he turned to make the twenty-mile trek back to me, I could see the men in the room lower their eyes as he passed. This room, en masse, was paying homage to a fallen warrior—one killed in the line of duty.

I wished then that I could have left my body and have floated over to the lady near the dance floor and asked her, "Hey, see that guy (me) with the curly hair standing over by the bar?"

"Yeah," she would say, looking in my direction.

"Well, if he came over and asked you to dance, would you say yes?"

In this version, she would look me up and down and say, "Yeah, why not?"

Now armed with *that* information, I'd swagger across the room, waving at all the guys. Smiling like a Cheshire cat, I'd simply hold out my hand and lead her to the dance floor. Done deal. With inside information, I would have a new confidence. If only there were a way to do that in sales. How can we know ahead of time if someone will buy or not *before* asking them to buy? If I had a tool like that I'd set sales records, I'd get up early and go to bed late, I'd double my income. There is such a tool. It's called X-Ray questions.

Well, just nine months later, my commissions were over $5,000 per month; I was driving a new Lincoln; and we had earned a trip to London, England. Things had changed.

Fishing for Leads

Want change? Want to grow? I'd like to take you on a trip, a fishing trip. And we will do like Jesus of Nazareth did with his disciples when he said, "I will make you fishers of men." That's exactly what we will do on this fishing trip. We will fish for leads.

Let's Define a Couple of Terms

fishing. The amount of time that you spend talking to someone who is not now using your product, service, or opportunity.

cutting bait. Everything else. Period.

Cutting bait is even the amount of time you spend organizing, doing inventory, or all of the necessary things that it takes to run a business. I want your total focus to be on getting new business. New blood. Do you have a problem in your business that doubling your volume wouldn't cure?

Drift Fishing, or How I Blew Lunch

I took my kids drift fishing in Hillsboro, Florida. Drift fishing is where a group of people get on a wide boat and motor out about a mile or so offshore and fish. It is called *drift* fishing because once the fishing begins, the captain shuts the motor off and the boat is allowed to drift and passengers are allowed to throw up. This activity ranks right up there with several poorly executed root canals. Anyway, we were out there about twenty minutes and no one has even had a nibble. We've done lots of chumming over the side but no fish. Even the guy named Buck, the one wearing one of those giant belt buckles, was busy heaving over the side. So the captain rang the bell, we hauled in our lines, and the boat proceeded south to a new spot. I had never done this before, so I turned around to one of the deck hands standing behind me and said, "Hey, where are we going?"

"To a better fishing hole," he said.

"What's wrong with this one?" I asked.

"You aren't catching anything!" he shouted.

"Then why did you bring us here?" I shouted back louder.

He looked at me with a wry grin and said, "Hey, shoulda been right here yesterday, pal . . . we got some huge ones!"

This didn't make me feel any better. But then he said something that we, as salespeople, tend to forget. He said, "We've got about five good fishin' holes up and down the coast . . . *because no fishing hole produces all the time.*"

And if we find a hole that is producing, we simply overfish the holes we have. Hardly anyone will sit next to us in choir anymore because we are constantly trying to do business. We even stoop to putting our business card in the offering plate so everyone gets to see it as it goes by. We will lose what few good fishing holes we have if we abuse them. We need at least seven good ones.

Cracker Jack and Uncle Sam

When I was about six years old, my brother Sam—*Sam Hill*, if you can believe that (my kids called him Uncle Sam)—took me outside one day and said, "Ricky, I have a surprise for you." It was a half-eaten box of Cracker Jack. Before he handed me the box, he took out my prize, opened it, and handed it to me. Who among us did not at one time or another get a small clear-plastic magnifying glass as the secret prize?

Sam had taken me outside to show me what I could do with my magnifying glass. Once outside, he set a piece of paper on the ground and looked up at the sky to find the sun and then focused the sunlight on the paper using the magnifying glass. He adjusted it just right so the beam of light was very bright and very small. Having done that, he just waited. And waited. To a six-year-old it seemed an eternity, but all of a sudden the paper started to turn brown around the beam of light. Then it started to smoke and, finally, fire! The paper actually caught fire, and my new toy had done it. Now that's a toy! So I was forbidden to play with matches, huh? Who cares? Sam left to play with his buddies, and I toddled off with my new toy. I went into the house, got a sheet of paper, and then went back outside to do what Sam had done. But with my level of hand-eye coordination, I couldn't hold the glass still enough to focus the beam. In my mind, I was doing *exactly* what Sam had done, but with different results.

Have you ever watched people in your profession grow very fast, even faster than you, and you copied everything they did, but for some odd reason you got very different results?

In your mind, you're doing *exactly* what they are doing. See, when I got into multilevel marketing, I thought I was doing exactly what my sponsor was doing, but I wasn't.

I'm going to ask you to focus now. Focus on one thing. Just *one* thing. You can't chase two rabbits at one time. For the next six months, I want you to concentrate on prospecting—getting new business by finding new people. For the next six months I don't want you to start painting your house or start any new project except getting new business for the business you are currently in. If you focus as well as my brother did with that beam of light, you'll get the right results. Record-breaking results! Keep reading and see.

PART II
Seven Fishing Techniques

Find Five Good Fishing Holes

Isn't it true that most salespeople find the most customers in the first few months of their careers? Even when they know the least? Is it true that most of us overfish the holes we have and never move on?

One of the biggest advertising houses in New York asks its future clients an important question, which most salespeople seldom ask.

Who buys your product?

The obvious answer to the question once you've been in business for a while is simply analyzing your purchase orders. Have you ever gone back over the purchase orders from the last two years and constructed a profile of your typical buyer? What are the average age, education, nationality, and religion? Where do these people hang out? Where do they worship? What clubs, associations, or professional groups do they join? What do they read? Which radio stations do they listen to? In other words, let's find them and go fishing. Advertising is designed to get them to come to you. Would you like a cheaper and more effective way? *Go to them.*

I was conducting a series of sales training meetings for one of Florida's largest manufacturers of yachts. These were major-league yacht builders. I asked the group who buys their boats (note to self:

say "Yachts" next time)? Almost in unison they answered, "Doctors. Doctors buy yachts."

I then asked how many of these yacht salespeople belonged to any medical associations? None. How many of them wrote articles on yachting for any medical trade journals? None. I then asked where the doctors in South Florida played golf or tennis? While it was varied, there were a few favorite places for doctors. To how many of these clubs would you guess these salespeople belonged? Right. None.

Back in 1975 I knew that most people who would want to get into the nutrition business were conservatives. I asked a few in the industry where they were recruited and not one was recruited in a singles bar. Not one at the dog track. Most were recruited at churches or temples, in neighborhoods, at health clubs, or small business association meetings. Many recruited their friends or relatives at these gatherings. So I went out and joined two health clubs, the local chamber of commerce and the Rotary Club. I also signed up for some ballroom dance lessons and joined a networking club. Some of these clubs and groups sounded like fun and some didn't. I joined Rotary because they do community service, and while I was there, I had a chance to find some new business. Let's vote. Right now, put this book down, get in your car, lay rubber out of the driveway, and go to your place of business. Unlock the door and quickly count the number of qualified buyers waiting for you. Shouldn't take long. Can you think of good round number? You can't fish at the office or at home. Sometimes I call distributors in my organization and say, "Hi. It's Rick . . . what's going on?" They say, "Oh hi, Rick. Just taking care of business . . ."

I say, "I'm confused. If you're taking care of business, how could you answer the phone? There isn't anyone *there* to do business *with*, is there?"

The biggest barrier you have to earning more money is not the economy or your competition or even the crummy sales manager or sponsor you have.

It's the *four walls of your office* (or home if you work from home).

Why is it that most new insurance and real estate agents and all others who have to generate their own leads do most of their business in the first 120 days and then quit? They fished all the holes they had. Then they started overfishing the same holes and then concluded that their business didn't work as well as they thought. Fact is, they simply overfished their fishing holes. Somebody needs to ring the bell, haul in the lines, and find new fishing holes.

It isn't enough just to join all these groups if you don't know what to look for and what to say. While some men use the chamber of commerce business card exchanges for hitting on good-looking ladies, business really can be conducted there if you have good technique.

When one first joins a club or association, the idea is to get involved. Get on a committee, do the newsletter, or plan events. Get known. Get some press. Get your picture in the newsletter as often as possible. Learn who the centers of influence are. These are the ones who influence the rest of the group's activity. Sell *them*, and you've got everyone else joining your team. Once you get to the fish, you must have bait they want—the kind of bait that nets big fish / big sales.

That's the subject of the next chapter.

Pop Quiz #1

1. Define "fishing."

2. Define "cutting bait."

3. What is the biggest barrier you have to getting new business?

4. How many fishing holes must one have?

Fishing for Leads

5. Why do we need more than one fishing hole?

   _____

   _____

6. List your top five fishing holes.

   a. _____

   b. _____

   c. _____

   d. _____

   e. _____

7. List five backup fishing holes (because the first five will go dry).

   a. _____

   b. _____

   c. _____

   d. _____

   e. _____

8. What does it mean to "overfish a fishing hole"?
_____
_____

9. What are the best two questions one can ask in marketing?
_____
_____

Change Your Bait

I had a good friend, a dentist in Grand Rapids, Michigan, who lived on a small lake and, before he passed away, when he wasn't asking someone to "open wide," fly-fished for relaxation. I saw him one day fly-fishing on the end of his dock. He'd swish the line back and forth with great purpose and style, and then he'd drop his fake fly near the shore, hoping a fish would think that it was the real thing. When he didn't catch anything for a while, he'd haul in his line and change baits. "Yep," he said in my direction, "if the fish don't want what ya got, change what ya got."

Good Zen-like stuff.

People who sell things get a lot of their business from networking or talking to the general public and getting referral business. We can catch a lot more business if the listener might want what we have. But even if they're hungry, if it doesn't *look or sound good* to them, they'll pass. My buddy Bob also tied flies. By that I mean he actually made fake bugs with a small hook cleverly hidden in the middle of multi-colored strings and feathers. Ever talk to a flytier? They are dead serious. Bob, for instance, had a small fortune in feathers, hides, string, hooks, and anything that could possibly look like a bug. His library was loaded with books that, and I'm not kidding, illustrated in full color the careful difference between a bug that looks sort of alive and one that looks like the real thing. If Bob throws a bug on the water that only looks sort of alive, he'll catch something that is sort of a fish. But if he did a good job of tying the fly and throws it to the right spot—dinner.

Sharpen Your Hook
Develop a One-Sentence Commercial

This is known also today as your elevator pitch. If you had to tell someone what you do between the first and tenth floors, could you do it and develop enough curiosity to make them ask questions? Develop a one-sentence commercial on what your prospect gets, not on what you do. That's it. When you are out in the public and someone asks you what you do for a living (just ask them to get them to ask you), what do you say? Most people in real estate say, "I'm a Realtor." Most people in the insurance business say, "I sell insurance."

All true. All dull. No bites.

How about this for real estate:

> "*You know what I really do? I teach people how to get the maximum amount of home for the minimum amount of monthly payment.*"

Hey, that's what people want. They want to live in a palace for free.

Try telling them *from their perspective* what it is that they get if they do business with you. Customize your "bait" to fit the crowd the same way an angler changes the bait to fit the fish in a particular fishing hole.

One thing more, try to include in your statement a word-picture. People think in terms of pictures, not words. The more vivid the graphic, the more impact it will have. Don't tell me what I might get—show me! With the proper gestures and voice inflection, you can make what they get, if they do business with you, bigger than life. If I were selling investments and my crowd was the thirty-something crowd, I'd say, "I teach people how to put their kids through school without affecting their monthly cash flow."

Tell them you are a stockbroker and you will be sipping your ginger ale alone. Last year in America, millions of hand drills were sold, yet not one person wanted an electric drill; everyone wanted a hole. I wouldn't sell vitamins; I would sell more energy. I wouldn't look for people who want to have a home-based business; I'd look for people who want to turn their homes into income-producing properties. Sell the ten-second commute. Make it live. Make it breathe. For crying out loud, tell people how their lives are about to change, not about how you fill *your* time!

Let me tell you what I learned about benefit statements. On paper, they all work. All of them, without exception, will make you a ton of money. On paper. But the marketplace is what determines viability. Take your little commercial to a chamber business card exchange and lay it on a few people. If their eyes glaze over and you are left munching on pigs in a blanket in the corner, get new bait because the fish aren't biting.

I have several benefit statements that I keep as different hooks or bait in my tackle box. Before I attend any kind of meeting I try and predict who will be there and select my bait accordingly. If I'm attending a support group for those with cancer, I use health-enhancing bait. If I'm attending a meeting of consultants, most of whom are unemployed, I use gig bait. Be just a little scientific here, but make sure it's bait that looks good to them. Once you have your one-sentence commercials designed, you can use those approaches to design closes and even company crusades!

When a prospective client calls me on my cell and asks what my program is about, the conversation usually goes something like this.

"Hello, this is Rick Hill speaking . . ."

"Is this Rick Hill?"

"Yes, it is . . ." (Didn't I just say it was?)

"Rick, this is Matt Dawson with the Dawson Insurance Group. A friend of mine heard you speak last week in Des Moines and said I should give you a call. We've got our annual meeting coming up in a couple of months, and I wondered what you talk about."

"Mr. Dawson," I say, "would it be helpful to your company if your salespeople could walk into a room full of people they've never met and walk out with several good prospects?"

"Rick, if you could get our troops doing that, we might have problems, but they wouldn't be financial."

"Good. I teach your associates seven solid fishing techniques to net new buyers. Give me three hours with your people and they'll be laying rubber out of the parking lot to go fishing for new business!"

"That sounds good . . . but I bet you're expensive . . ."

"Let me do this," I say. "Let me complete a booking agreement with the dates, times, place, transportation costs, lodging and meals, and speaking fee—if any. If it all looks good when you get it, just initial the agreement and send it back with a 50 percent deposit check, and booking this meeting is off your plate."

Sounds easy, right? It is if you have your one-sentence commercial down cold. It has been my experience that most companies are not focused enough to have a one-sentence banner under which they march. I did this seminar for a management company with just seven of their vice presidents attending. I gave them some samples of good "bait" statements. The meeting started at eight in the morning. When we broke for lunch at one o'clock they were still haggling over one sentence. The discipline of defining what people get when they do business with you is a powerful marketing tool for your company.

An even more disciplined and shorter version of an elevator speech is the Bumper Sticker theme. It's harder to create because it can only be a few words or a short slogan. There was a plastic bag manufacturer in Fort Lauderdale that was located very near I-95. They had a large lighted sign on the side of their building that read, **Bags on Time.** I like that. I know *what* they make and *how fast* I will get it, in just three words. Clean, and to the point.

What do you do? When you do the hard work of distilling your efforts into one clear sentence, you also have a marketing theme.

Since I do two programs, I have two hook statements I use when I'm out and about recruiting.

1. Benefit Statement for *Fishing for Leads*
   "I teach your people how to walk into a room full of people they've never met and walk out with new prospects."
2. Benefit Statement for *The Cancer Conundrum*
   "I beat terminal cancer thirty-eight years ago by hitting my Reset button, and I teach people how to find and hit theirs."

Most hook statements are long, wordy, and sound as if old cigar-chomping attorneys put the thing together while they were on the clock. Put it in the language of the street your prospect lives on. Short. No big words. The way people think and talk.

Once we find good fishing holes and have good bait, everyone finds out that lots of trips to the fishing holes are necessary. Sometimes, "Why prospect?" can be as good a question as "How do I prospect?"

Pop Quiz #2

1. A good hook statement tells people what they _____, not what you _____.

2. Why should a company buy from you?
   _____
   _____

3. Write out your one-sentence commercial or hook statement.
   _____
   _____

4. What do you ask someone to get them to ask you what you do?
   _____
   _____

5. Name three people on whom you dropped your hook statement this week.

   a. _____

   b. _____

   c. _____

Fishing With Purpose
Your Mission Statement

Have you ever hit a slump in your sales career? Have you ever gotten to the point where you hit the snooze button till noon? Have you ever watched movies instead of making sales calls or networking? No? Well, I have. I've never met a straight commission salesperson that didn't lose his or her motivation at some point. So this next section is for anyone out there who has ever mentally thrown in the towel. Fishing needs to be synonymous with connecting what you are doing with a larger purpose—a mission.

During World War II, the Germans conducted a terrible but instructive experiment. The Allies had bombed one of their labor camps housing our POWs. Several of the main buildings were destroyed, but luckily for the prisoners the barracks were not hit. The next morning the prisoners were forced to move the rubble, brick by brick, from one side of the compound to the other. The following day they were made to take it back, brick by brick, to the original site. No explanation, no reason given. This went on for several weeks and the prisoners started getting sick. After a couple of months, they started dying, some by suicide. The indignity of laboring without a purpose of any kind killed their human spirit.

One bright winter day many years ago, two woodsmen were out chopping trees down in the forest. One said to the other, "Hey, I'll give you a hundred dollars if you turn your axe around and use the flat side for the rest of today."

"Just turn it around and I get a hundred bucks?" the surprised lumberjack asked. "Done!" he said.

So he turned his axe around and began whacking at the tree. Several hours later he walked over to his friend and said, "Keep your hundred bucks. I gotta see the chips fly."

William James, the great American psychologist, said that humans get most of their sense of well-being from their work, not from their relationships or possessions. Your hook is clearly defining *why* you do what you do, not just what you do. There is great power in connecting your daily activities to a larger purpose. Let me quickly tell you my story because most of you will see yourselves somewhere in this illustration.

I became a Shaklee distributor of natural food supplements and other health-related products on June 21, 1975. As I said earlier, I had undergone surgery at the Mayo Clinic for stage III cancer.

I left Mayo's and went to Dr. Contreras's clinic, the *Oasis of Hope*, for the B17 treatments. While I was there I learned a great deal about diet, nutrition, and the use of whole-food vitamin supplements in building your body's immune system. I also learned about using other kinds of products, like toothpaste or shampoo, which are natural and organic and deliver fewer harmful chemicals to your body. Adopting this diet, food-supplement regimen, and using these personal care products allowed me to get away from eating fake food and using harmful chemicals on a daily basis. As a follow-up to my clinic experience in Mexico, I stuck to the same approach at home, and that, in time, led me into the food-supplement business.

This business gave me a unique opportunity to help other people achieve better health. It gave me a chance to offer people hope. A friend of mine, Mike Johanneck, defined hope like this:

H-elping

O-ther

P-eople

E-scape

I like that. What a crusade, what a raison d'etre! I was working with a magnificent obsession. I was not only making more money than I had ever made, but I was also helping people find their way to vibrant health. They were eating differently, stopping smoking, and abandoning other health-destroying habits. In just forty-one months I had earned the top title at Shaklee. In addition, I was enjoying a six-figure income and perks like a company car and paid convention trips to exotic locations.

Oddly enough, the day I earned my top title, I lost interest. For one thing, I was too young to appreciate what I had done or had earned. I was twenty-seven years old, which at that time was the youngest in the company's thirty-year history. I thought to myself, "Okay, now what? Just because I'm good at it doesn't mean I have to do it the rest of my life, does it?"

So I quit. Most of those I had recruited into the same business felt disappointed and a bit abandoned. Some quit when I did. I spent the next ten years developing new skills. I wrote several books, was a satire columnist for Knight-Ridder newspapers, was a talk show host for WSBR in Boca Raton, served a term as president of the

Florida Speakers Association, and was vice president of a professional speaking company called Mentalrobics. All good things, eh?

Something was missing. I was busy. It was all very interesting. But for me, it did not give me the same emotional return as when I'd see someone regain lost health or do well as a new distributor. Before, I was changing lives. I had a story to tell, *my* escape. I used my story to help *them* escape.

So in 2012 I decided to rebuild my speaking business and get back on the road. The Free Speakers Group was born.

At this point, I gotta ask ya, what's your hook? If you read about the lives of successful entrepreneurs, a common thread is that they attached what they were doing to a larger picture. Here's a wonderful statement that Gary Burke gave me one day: *glance at circumstances, stare at purpose.*

In the early days of my career when I wasn't doing very well, the *circumstances* were that we were broke, but my *purpose* in giving other people hope kept me going. When I was at the Oasis Clinic the circumstances were that I was dying, but my purpose to *reset* my life was strong enough that I took the risk of pursuing an unconventional method of treating cancer. We, of all the creatures of the earth, are driven by purpose.

Here is the place for your mission statement. This should be written in language that is meaningful to you. It's for your ears and your heart only. It's the line to which you cling when your career ship seems to be taking on water. It's the truth you repeat to yourself when the fish don't seem to be biting but the bills don't seem to notice. It's your thought when you come home and your husband or wife says sarcastically, "Sell anything today?" It's your beacon, your lighthouse, and your plumb bob. Here's our mission statement:

Our Programs Are Free and We Quit on Time!

I have this statement included in my written annual goals. The large turnover many companies experience may be due to the fact that there is no company crusade. Let me ask you, what is your company crusade? What larger purpose can there be if you sell something common? Ask Harvey McKay. He manufactures and sells envelopes, something that is common to everyone and is easily copied. But he sees his efforts as part of a larger picture. He visualizes his part in making the US economy healthy and competitive. He uses his money to promote civic and charitable events in Minnesota. He simply connects his daily activities to a much broader purpose.

Loyalty can be a hook. A company's hook is what holds employees even when times are tough. Companies that don't have a hook often have a difficult time keeping people over the long haul.

With good fishing holes, good bait, and a sharp hook, it's time to find hungry fish.

Finding Hungry Fish

Have you ever seen people go to a chamber of commerce meeting and, after having gotten their carrot sticks and ginger ale, just stand around grinning at everybody, wondering why they don't get more new business? They go home and tell their spouse, "No one talked to me . . ." It does little good to go to networking activities if you don't know what to do when you arrive. Or worse, have you been to one of these activities and had some evangelistic multilevel disciple "fire hose" you with glowing tales of getting rich overnight?

The number one characteristic of the novice salesperson is to say too much, too soon.

I've had so-called professional salespeople call on me at my office and, once they were seated, go on relentlessly about the features, advantages, and benefits of their product. They never once asked me what I wanted. Would you like a simple method of walking into a room full of people that you have never met and walk out with several prospects? You can. Here's how.

Questions are the key to more prospects. Not just any questions, but *x-ray* questions. X-ray questions give you more information about a prospect than you might ordinarily get in casual conversation. Good questions give you that inside information so you don't get your head chopped off. With the right questions you can know ahead of time if your prospect might even be remotely interested in what you're selling. This does not mean that you get every sale. It does mean that you deal with less rejection, and to a professional salesperson, that has value.

Let's say, for instance, that you want to recruit someone into your insurance firm. When you walk into a room full of people you can't know ahead of time who might be interested and who isn't. But with just a few questions you can find out. Let me give you a scenario that I've played out many times, and then we'll go back and study some of it. Sounds something like this.

"Jim," I say to the person standing next to me at the Rotary meeting, "what do you do when you're not here?"

"Oh, I play a lot of tennis, golf some, and I'm in real estate."

"How long have you been doing real estate?"

"About fifteen years, I guess."

"Fifteen years!" I say with some astonishment in my voice. "You must love it to be in it that long!"

"Well," he says, clearing his throat, "to tell you the truth, I think it's time to look for something else. The market went into the toilet and I just need a change."

"Have you found anything yet?"

"No, not really," he says with some sadness. "My brother-in-law wants me to go into a new business with him . . . something about multileveling Teflon underwear . . ."

"I see," I say with a straight face, "and how's that going?"

"I'd never go into business with him! He's a real jerk."

"Well," I say, looking perplexed, "what are you going to do?"

"Don't really know, just keep looking, I guess."

"Listen," I say with deep-furrowed brows, "my business is growing and I'm always looking for good people. Let's meet this week and I'll give you the details."

Now the main point from this sample conversation is that I opened it with an x-ray question: "What do you do when you're not here?" That is a user-friendly way of saying, "What do you do for a living and do you like it?" When they tell me, I ask them how long they've been doing it and compliment them on their career by saying, "Wow, you must really love it!" Few people love what they do. Few people can take a compliment well. Ever tell a lady that her dress was smashing? What did she say?

"This old rag?"

If a man ever complimented a woman on her dress and she responded, "Thank you, but if you think this dress is nice, you ought to see what I'm wearing underneath it!" He would faint. When they respond with little enthusiasm to my compliment, I know I've got a chance. Here is where we separate the champions from the "also-rans."

Do not fire hose your prospect.

I was training a young guy in Fort Lauderdale, and we had to fly to Tampa for an appointment. So we are seated on the plane and a guy sits next to my trainee, who is happily reading his morning newspaper. My guy says, "Hi! I'm Fred!"

The guy drops his paper and stares at Fred with dread on his face. Fred doesn't miss a beat and says, "I can teach you how to make a fortune. If you ever swallowed a vitamin, you've been trained . . . here's . . ."

Fred proceeds to regurgitate all he has ever known about the world of nutrition and selling on this poor guy. When Fred slows down just a bit, the guy snaps his paper back up between himself and Fred, and the conversation ended. Fred looked back at me and winked like he's just hit a grand slam at Fenway Park.

When we got off of the plane, Fred turned to me, grinning like a kid in a candy store, and said, "How'd I do?" I pretended I was holding a fire hose and made the gushing sound.

Less is more. Like John Travolta always said in his *Get Shorty* films when asked what he was going to say, "As little as possible, if that . . ."

When many salespeople find a crack in their prospect's armor, they fire hose their prospect with tons of useless information. Your job is to widen the crack, open a vein, and get their heads under water until you no longer see bubbles. Until people admit they're lost, they cannot be found. Until they admit they are drowning, they cannot be rescued. Get them to tell you just how bad it is, how it got that way, and that they don't have a clue about how to solve it. You are killing objections before objections can be raised with good x-ray questions.

In over thirty years of professional selling, I have never found a more key principle than learning the art of interviewing. During the two years I did talk radio at WSBR in Boca, my biggest lesson was learning to listen, really listen and *dilate* problems. Make mountains out of molehills. Let me say it once more: saying too much too soon is the mark of a novice. Interviewing before you present is the mark of a champion.

Try this: just interview at first. Take two weeks and don't worry about trying to get the appointment or sale. Just get good at interviewing without the pressure of trying to close. You might find that some of the fish will jump in the boat without being asked. Less is more. The more relaxed I am, the more I seem to attract the right people and situations.

Getting good at fishing yet? Now it's time to catch bunches of fish!

Pop Quiz #3

1. To sharpen your hook, what is your larger purpose in business?

_____

_____

2. Please give your mission statement (not your hook statement).

_____

_____

3. What is the number one characteristic of the novice salesperson?

_____

_____

4. Define "x-ray" questions.

_____

_____

5. Define "fire hosing" people.

_____

_____

6. Name three people you "fire hosed" this week.

    a. _____

    b. _____

    c. _____

Fishing with Nets

Every good angler knows that if you are going to go from a hobby to making a living, you must learn to fish with nets. Wouldn't it be nice to recruit bunches of new customers instead of one at a time? Mass advertising and mass mailing were the main methods to accomplish this in the past, but since the Internet, one cannot survive without a website and a general understanding of Internet marketing. Want a way to fish with nets that costs very little? The good news is that these nets not only don't cost very much but also work like crazy, if you are willing to run the risk of speaking and writing.

If you are willing to become a better public speaker, you can fish with nets and reach hundreds of prospects a month for virtually nothing in cost. If you are willing to learn about the Internet and social media, you can extend your reach far beyond your having to be there to make the connection. Doing free speeches and using the Internet are two excellent ways to fish with nets.

Things Had Changed

Early in the spring of 1957, when the whole countryside was bursting with life, a little seven-year-old boy made up his mind that he would never talk to anyone ever again. Many kids say similar things when they have been angered, but this little guy went nearly a whole year without speaking. You see, he stuttered so badly that the effort just wasn't worth it. In addition to that he slurred his "S" sounds so that most of the kids in the neighborhood thought he sounded like Daffy Duck. Children don't usually mean to be cruel, but they can be brutally honest, and they usually were when they mimicked him. In fact, when they could get him mad enough, he would try to shout back at them, which only made things far worse because he would get stuck on a word like "you" (as in, "You're going to get it!") and just turn bright red trying to say the word. Of course, the redder he got, the louder they laughed.

One day he went bowling with his brothers and sister. They were all having a great time when, during one of his times to bowl, the ball accidentally slipped from his hand and landed with a loud crash in the next lane. Everyone laughed and laughed at the expressions on the faces of the people in that lane. Later that afternoon when they returned home, everyone started to tell their father about the incident at the bowling alley. Someone yelled, "Hey, quit telling his story . . . let him tell it."

Suddenly everyone remembered that this little guy had not spoken in months, and now every eye in the room was watching to see what would happen. Almost forgetting his speechless days, he was just so excited about the incident that he began telling the story. But when he got to the word "ball," he got stuck. After trying several times to start over, he turned bright red and just put his little head down and gave up . . . he just gave up. No one knew what to do or say. It was so deathly quiet in the room.

I remember that incident so well because that little boy was me.

I guess one of the reasons I wrote this book is that I remember all of that so well. I know what it is to have something worthwhile to say and not be able to say it.

By contrast, here's what happened to me in the spring of 1981. Fort Worth, Texas, was buzzing with activity. There was a big network marketing convention downtown at the Civic Auditorium, and cars and motor homes were everywhere, trying to find a place to park. Being the last speaker that day, I faced a very tired and crowded audience of over ten thousand people. But when I was done, the crowd stood to their feet in a thunderous ovation. I walked to the edge of the stage to bow and receive their applause, and fought back tears as I remembered back to 1957. Things had changed.

The Importance of Public Speaking

Even a good speaker at times knows what to say but just can't "get it out." This book is designed to help you organize your thoughts and deliver those thoughts very nearly as they are in your mind. One reason that you should read this book is that I have struggled a great deal to be an accomplished public speaker. Because I did have some obstacles to overcome, it made me take every step one at a time. In simple words, I sat where you sat.

I can just hear what you are saying in your mind, "Yes, but isn't the ability to be a good speaker a gift?" Have you ever heard someone say, "She is really a gifted speaker?" Yes, I have heard that expression, and yes, I believe that public speaking is a gift to a certain degree. While I do believe that I have the gift of speaking, I also believe that many people do. It goes undeveloped because of fear and a sheer lack of desire.

The emotion of fear is the strongest motivator, but desire happens to be a close second. Before you even read the rest of this book, ask yourself this question, "How strong is my desire to be an accomplished speaker?"

With me it became a magnificent obsession, thinking about it constantly, working long hours on speeches, and then literally years of practice. My memories of long hours alone in the basement (so no one could hear me) reciting over and over "Sister Sally sat by the seashore selling shells" are so vivid after more than 50 years. I used to tape-record myself reading and notice which words would make me stutter and which "S" sounds were the most difficult to change. For one speech I gave in the eighth grade for the Optimists Club contest, I prepared for over a month just to be certain I could pronounce all of the S sounds and wouldn't trip over any words, and over time, I got better. I estimate that I have given two thousand speeches in the years preceding the writing of this book. Just the fact that you bought this book indicates to me that you want to improve too. People who have no gift at all usually have no desire at all. I just *knew* I had the potential to be a good speaker—it's just that no one had any reason to agree with me for a long time. Your desire and effort can and will take you far beyond the "natural speaker" who never reaches his or her potential because of fear or lack of desire.

My Format for Speech Writing

While attending college, my best friend, Russ Pehl, was the captain of the wrestling team. He was a magnificent athlete who, as I recall, was rarely beaten. He would have won the state championship in high school if he hadn't broken his arm in the final match. Having grown up in a nonaffluent suburb of Detroit, I had never seen a real college wrestling match. We had the professional type of stuff on TV, complete with rabbit punches and faces being mashed into the turnbuckles. When I went away to college I finally saw my first college match. Wow, was I impressed.

The next day I joined my college wrestling team. In order to wrestle on the A squad, I had to defeat a guy named Paul Clark, who was ranked third in the state of Oklahoma. Well, I developed some very impressive calluses on my shoulder blades and on my kneecaps but could never beat Paul in order to wrestle for the A squad. Russ approached me one day and said, "Rick, if you want to be a better wrestler, let me give you some advice. Learn *one* good takedown, *one* good reverse, and *one* good pin hold. Learn these so well that you could do them on most anyone you wrestle. Most guys want to learn fifteen different takedowns because it is monotonous practicing one move again and again. But then they never really get proficient at any of them. You won't become a national champion with only three perfected moves, but you'll win more than you do now."

Let me apply that good advice to public speaking. There are three basic parts to any speech.

1. Introduction
2. Body
3. Conclusion

I can hear you saying that this information comes under the heading of "so what?" I know that's not big news. But if you could learn a *format*, a *process* for developing a speech, it could make you a far better speaker. Most people never learn a good method of opening a talk, of varying the rise and fall of the body content and delivery, and an effective way to close. They have never learned a system that works for any subject and type of speech. Such a system not only exists but I will also teach it to you. You paid for it. And the best news is that it works. I know—I use it!

Move #1: The Takedown
Introductions That Claim Attention

Let me relate one of my Bill Gove sessions with you for illustration. Bill would attend a speech I was giving in the area and sit in the back taking notes. It was nerve-racking to watch him writing like crazy, but I wanted to get better, so I just went with it.

I went bounding up to him after the speech and said, "Well, how'd I do?"

He said, "I never critique a speech the day it's given. Let's meet for lunch at my country club and I'll go over it." And with that, he left.

Several days later we had lunch at the 18th Hole Café (almost every golf club has one). Once our sandwiches and iced tea arrived, Bill took out his notes and said, standing up, "Okay, here's the way you started your speech . . ."

And right there, in front of the whole restaurant, he walked to the entry door, announced me as the speaker, and then he pretendsed to be me walking in and gave a few of my opening remarks. No one in the club even paid any attention because they were used to his antics.

When he was done, he continued by saying, "Here's what you could have said," and then gave my introduction the way *he* would have.

His main point was don't attack the group. Ask the guy in the front row how his back is doing. How do you know his back is bad? "Everyone over fifty has back trouble," Bill says. "It never misses." Then he starts low in volume and slow in pace so he has somewhere to go with volume and emphasis. Bill Gove talks *to* the crowd, not *at* them.

I was once a part of our church choir. Now church choirs are the brunt of many jokes because they are generally pretty lousy. Almost anyone can join, and each piece has very limited time in preparation. We used to joke about our opening and closing. If we all stood together and started singing exactly together on the downbeat, people were impressed. Then at the end, in a rousing, crashing crescendo, if we cut off instantly without leaving Mrs. McDuffy warbling alone, the congregation was really wowed. We could be off-key and off rhythm and be singing from the wrong page during the middle but a good clean start and a big, even finish still brought down the house.

The introduction and conclusion of your speech are the most important parts. There are two main purposes for the beginning of your speech:

1. To get acquainted with your audience
2. To state your proposition

After I have been introduced and have confidently approached the microphone, I always pause momentarily. This is the time that I use to relax and get my audience to relax by just chatting with them a few minutes about the convention or the meals or whatever has happened. I try to think of something humorous that has happened during the course of the meeting or take off on something one of the speakers had said in his or her talk. Again my motive is to relax the audience, not to make another speaker on the program look like a jerk. It's also a time to thank the sponsors of the convention and to express your appreciation for everyone who has made the special effort to attend. I let the audience know that they made a wise choice to attend and that it's going to be exciting. This can be done without bragging.

Now let's look at an ironclad rule in relation to the introduction. It is worth repeating a thousand times.

Never apologize about being the speaker. Never.

I have heard the mousiest, most timid, milquetoast introductions that were all given in the name of modesty and humility. That's just silly. You're a professional. If you weren't you wouldn't have been asked or shouldn't have been. Here are some introductions to avoid:

"I'm really not a speaker but . . ."
"I have a bad cold, so please bear with me . . ."
"I'm not as good as the last speaker, but I'll do my . . ."
"This is my first big meeting so bear with me . . ."

Listen, people do not drive hours and hours, pay admission, sit on hard chairs, and strain their necks and eyes for two solid hours to "bear with" anyone. Get excited about the value you can be to your audience.

If the person who spoke before you is better than you are, try something like this: "Wow! Betty, that was one of the finest talks I have ever heard. That really was great, and today I want to share the three most challenging aspects of my business career. This all made sense to me after I learned that . . ."

Or just don't say anything about the former speaker. But if you follow a speaker, it is usually expected that you will make some comment. If the speaker before you was really dull or obnoxious, then just comment on the general success of the conference and how each speaker has taught you valuable information (even if it was how *not* to do something). Resist the temptation to say, "Okay, let's get things moving again here" or "Let's all stand now and wake up!" or "Haven't most of the speakers been great?"

An important thing to do in the first few moments in the talk is to establish eye contact. I use and have long been a promoter of something that most speakers are afraid to use. Yet to me it is the *single most important tool* of public speaking, and everyone, I mean everyone, can do it from the time they are born. If you can learn to use this tool you will instantly improve your speaking abilities.

Wait for it . . .

Wait for it . . .

SILENCE

Waiting, though not as irritating as this was, creates anticipation. Even the typing of the word above caught your eye, not because of what was typed but because of the spaces in which nothing was typed. It's the pause, the space that people need to reflect on. The vast use of expressions like "uh" and "er" and "know what I mean?" is based on an erroneous assumption, namely, that any silence is a sign of forgetting or being unprepared. In one of my talks that were videotaped in Florida, I paused after what I considered an important statement and just vacuumed up eye contact. Later when I had a chance to review the tape, I timed that pause by my watch, and it lasted a full eight seconds. Silence is a very powerful tool. That five-to-ten-second pause when you collect everyone's attention is important. I heard a pilot tell how his single-engine plane went dead high over a major city. He said later, "I will never forget the sound of that dead engine. The silence was deafening."

After recognitions and appreciations are given and eye contact and quiet are achieved, it's time for your statement of proposition.

The Proposition

Tells Everyone Where You Are Headed

A speech without a proposition is a rudderless, goalless mass of answers to questions no one is asking. The proposition is your goal;

it's your statement of purpose. It can take the form of a question, a statement of fact, or even a short story. But it must be clear and concise.

A proposition can be very effective in the form of a bold statement. One sales leader allegedly opened a talk at a major convention with the following words, "Hello, liars . . ." Short and to the point, and no one forgot that speech. That speaker was addressing the problem of people who exaggerate the truth to make it appear better than it is.

I usually state a problem in my proposition and then solve it in my speech. I began one this way.

"Six years ago today I was told by a Mayo Clinic physician that I had a short time to live. Today, I want to share with you three ways I conquered cancer naturally and how those three ways can also prevent cancer."

The Transitional Sentence

Tells Everyone HOW You Intend to Arrive

The transitional sentence is the bridge that takes you from your statement of purpose or direction to the main body of content.

For example, "In the short time we have together, I'd like to teach you about detoxification, supplementation, and affirmation as the three ways to possibly avoid cancer."

Move #2: The Switch

The body of your speech is what develops the proposition.

Your outline should not have more than three main points. Humans can remember long outlines. Once, I heard Bill Gove imitate a bad speaker when he said, "Today, I'm going to speak about goal setting, and in order to do that, I've picked the acronym MESOPOTAMIA... M is for..." And suddenly, the entire room looks at their watch in shock. If your outline has three major points, you need three good stories to illustrate those points, and humorous incidents make good illustrative material.

Sample Propositional Outline

Are You Sure You Can't Do This Business?

Proposition Many people feel defeated from the start in their businesses because they are playing the comparison game. It's deadly. They compare themselves with others and believe they do not have the same abilities.

Transitional Sentence I want to take you step by step through the most common excuses people use and knock them down one by one. You will, I believe, leave here thinking to yourself, "Boy, if that klutz can make a go of this business, then I sure can."

Move #3: The Pin Hold
Closes That Leave the Crowd Wanting More

The best conclusions have a simple format.

1. Restate the proposition
2. Tell a final story with emotional impact that reflects the truth of your proposition as nothing else can. As one man said of outlining: *Introduction*: "Tell 'em what you're gonna tell 'em."
Body: "Tell 'em."
Conclusion: "Tell 'em what ya told 'em."

Celebrate success at the end of your speech; you earned it.

You worked for it. Listen to the sound of that applause, feel the vibration coming from the audience. Observe the approval and enthusiasm in their faces and look for renewed hope and confidence in their expressions. That's why you came.

Let me ask you something: How good are you at what you do? Really? Who knows about it? Do you have a specific skill or information that someone would pay $10,000 for it over a year's time and believe that they got a bargain? There are people reading this book who are experts in their chosen field. They are darn good at what they do, maybe better than anyone else. The real question is, who knows about it? I'm going to ask you to become a PR person. I want you to become your own public relations agent.

If you are promoting a particular product, do not directly promote it if you want to get published. For example, if I were a Realtor and I wanted to get listings, I'd write an article entitled "How to Showcase Your Home for More Money." At the end of the article I'd have my company name and contact information. My article to promote nutritional products is entitled "How I Conquered Cancer with Nutrition." It does not mention the brand name of the vitamins I sell but does have my name and contact information at the end of the article.

Every community has tons of associations. People band together for everything and often form associations. Ask your local chamber of commerce for a list of clubs and associations. Some are the oddest groups—*The Daughters of the Sisters of the Husbands Who Fought in the Alamo and Thought They Won but Didn't.* Every association has two basic things: a rubber chicken luncheon and a newsletter. You can attend the luncheons and network and you can write articles for their newsletter.

If your interest is increasing as you read this book and you want more information, there are several ways you can do this.

1. Read my book—you've almost done that.
2. Log on to free webinars listed on our website: http://www.freespeakersgroup.com
3. Log on to our website and register for our promotions and events.

On the next few pages, you will see samples of my Free Speakers flyer, bio, and Introduction that I send to all of the associations and the outline and order form I put on every chair. The outline and order form also has our website, information on products and services, and an invitation to log on to a future webinar for more information at no cost.

If your next speaker cancels,
my 20 minutes is free and I quit on time!

Rick Hill presents...

Fishing for Leads

Fishing for Leads will teach you how to

- Find 5 Good Fishing Holes
- Develop one sharp hook
- Weigh your catch
- Fish with nets

Book Rick for your next event!

Rick is sponsored by: *FreeSpeakersGroup.com*

There is no charge to book him for your next event.

According to Rick, "If you want to create a never ending chain of referrals, this works! And, *I quit on time!*"

Contact: Rick @ rickh@freespeakersgroup.com

Rick Hill Bio

Rick's career in sales and marketing began one cold November morning in November of 1968 at 10,000 feet in a Beechcraft Bonanza. That was the first time Rick heard Earl Nightingale's *Lead the Field* series of cassette tapes— and his life has not been the same since.

Suddenly Rick discovered he had terminal cancer in 1974 and conquered it at www.OasisofHope.com. From this experience, Rick began selling and marketing vitamins and become the youngest top sales leader in Shaklee's 30 year history. Several years later, he resigned and started his own nutritional company recruiting over 1,500 sales people personally.

During his tenure as VP of Sales for the Shaklee Corporation, Hill personally sold $25,000,000 in big-ticket items from the platform. Learn from the best, learn from a record-holder, learn from Rick Hill how to walk into a room full of people you've never met, and walk out with new business!

Rick is sponsored by: **The Free Speakers Group**
There is no charge to book him for your next event.
According to Rick, "The information and entertainment value might double your volume... and, *I quit on time!*"

Contact: rickh@freespeakersgroup.com

Rick Hill Introduction

Our Speaker today, Rick Hill began his career in sales and marketing began one cold November morning in November of 1968 at 10,000 feet in a Beechcraft Bonanza. That was the first time Rick heard Earl Nightingale's *Lead the Field* series of cassette tapes—and his life has not been the same since.

Suddenly Rick discovered he had terminal cancer in 1974 and conquered it at www.OasisofHope.com. From this experience, Rick began selling and marketing vitamins and become the youngest top sales leader in Shaklee's thirty-year history. Several years later, he resigned and started his own nutritional company recruiting over 1,500 sales people personally.

During his tenure as VP of Sales for the Shaklee Corporation, Hill personally sold $25,000,000 in big-ticket items from the platform. Learn from the best, learn from a record-holder, learn from Rick Hill how to walk into a room full of people you've never met, and walk out with new business!

Hill is a Master Prospector and can increase your bottom line!

Help me welcome, all the way from El Cajon, CA, Rick Hill!

Pop Quiz #4

1. What are the two chief methods of "Fishing with Nets"?

   _____

   _____

2. Give the three parts of every speech.

   _____

   _____

   _____

3. A good introduction does what two things?

   _____

   _____

4. Never ever apologize for what?

   _____

5. What is the single greatest tool in public speaking?
_____

6. What is the main purpose of the proposition in a speech?
_____

7. What does the transitional sentence do?
_____

_____

8. The best conclusion does what two things?
_____

_____

9. What should you always do at the very end of your speech?
_____

Weigh Your Catch
The Qualification Process

There are four basic parts to the sales process.

1 Prospecting
2 Qualifying
3 Closing
4 Service

The qualifying that must come after prospecting is the hardest to teach and the most controversial. Let me make a statement and see what you think.

The basis of my success was really who I didn't work with.

Here's why: without qualifying a customer or prospect, you can unconsciously recruit time vampires or people who are all hat and no cattle. In the beginning of my business, I wanted distributors so badly that I would practically do all their work for them. They would call and want to shoot the breeze for hours, and they just weren't producing.

So I changed the way I did business. Between 1976 and 1979, I set a record in the Shaklee field that has never been broken. Yet I was far from the tallest, best-looking, or most charismatic person in the field. How did I do it? In a sentence, I qualified my prospects before investing any time, energy, or money into them.

In that business, my hook statement, when someone asked me what I did, was to say, "I found these vitamins that really worked for me, and if they work half as well for you, it could be worth some serious income for you . . ."

If they asked, "How does that work?"

I'd answer, "Really well!"

They'd grin and I'd say, "I'm not set up right now to give you the best information, but if you'd like to grab a quick cup of coffee this week, I'd be happy to meet you again and go over it."

The point there was I didn't fire hose them or try and sell on a street corner.

Once I meet with someone and show him (or her of course) an opportunity, I tell him a short story:

I've been in this business a very long time. I've never been able to tell if someone is going to be successful or not. But I have studied the lives of the very successful in our company, and to a person they all do three things consistently.

1. *They use all our products.* If you continue to use competitor's products it sends a double message. Are you willing to use all our products? He may say, "Well no, I like such and such from another company." I say, "No problem. Listen, if you change your mind about that, call me, and we'll get some work done."

He says, "You mean you won't work with me unless I use all your products?" To which I answer, "Well, it's not so much that as it is you'll fail and I'll get blamed."

2. *You need to get a list of people that we can contact.*

He may say, "No, Buffy and I went to Harvard and we are just going to open an Internet site and let it do the work . . ."

Once again, I thank him and tell him if he changes his mind to call me.

So I'd go through several things that he needed to do or I wouldn't work with him. Only one in five was willing to do all of them, but when he did, I knew I had a qualified prospect and wasn't wasting my time. Most people want success for other people worse than they want it for themselves. Qualifying is done through activity, not promises or goals.

3. *Invite your five best prospects to a business meeting—you invite, I'll speak.*

Lots of people don't like meetings. My position has always been that it is hard to develop loyalty or fellowship without them. Get hired at IBM and tell them you prefer not to attend any meetings. See how that goes.

Most of this book deals with prospecting. However, the qualifying process determines how much fishing has to be done. If you keep throwing your fish back, you need to stay out there longer so you have enough qualified prospects to make your goals. As a general rule, people do not qualify prospects because they do not want to keep prospecting. They are afraid to throw one back because they are afraid they might not catch another one.

This is especially true in a multilevel business. Most sales leaders in multilevel companies are working with people who are not fully committed. Before I got started in multilevel, my sponsor showed me a commitment sheet that gave me a realistic idea of what it would take to get started. His closing statement was, *"When you stop, I stop."*

Most of us want success so badly that we are willing to make calls for our people, run their meetings, and even swallow their vitamins if we could. My sponsor, Gary Burke, qualified people through activity. On this subject he said, "If they balk on any of these major issues, I welcomed them to the organization as wholesale buyers and assured them I'd give them great service, and if they should ever change their minds about working the business, I'd be ready to work with them. But I'm not going to chase people who are unwilling to do the basics."

By the way, the scope of this book does not cover the art of Closing a sale or Service. But in a couple of sentences, the best close of all for me is simply, "Would you like to know how to get started?" Neat and clean! The best way to give good service is this comment my manager gave to me, "What you do to get 'em, you've got to keep doing to keep 'em."

Using The Internet and Social Media to Fish with Nets

In 1993, when I first wrote *The Fishing Trip*, CBS did a documentary on the new invention called the Internet. Imagine that. When I first conceived of teaching people what I had learned about prospecting, there was no one I knew who had a website or had any concept whatsoever of social media. The world has changed radically since then.

For purposes of this particular discussion, let's focus on a couple of aspects that are popularly used today—search engines, websites, and Facebook, which, by the way, was only launched in 2004 on college campuses.

To illustrate useful methods of using these media, let me show you how I found buyers for this new book in 2012. Of course I used all of the methods outlined in the previous chapters of this book:

1. *I found five good fishing holes.*
   a. Joined the chamber of commerce in El Cajon
   b. Joined the Optimists Club of El Cajon
   c. Did free speeches at Rotary, Optimists, and other civic groups
   d. Had a book launch event at two eateries in Rancho San Diego
   e. Piggybacked any event for Beat Cancer meetings and offered this book as a bonus book.
2. *I needed some new tools to reach new people.*
   a. I needed a new website to promote my book.
   b. I needed to find a dozen affiliate partners.
   c. Set a date for a Media Blitz.
   d. Set a goal to reach five thousand new people on launch day via Facebook.

Sound doable? It is, and it is a lot of work. Let's take them one at a time and I can highlight what I've learned.

Websites are not nearly as intimidating as they were five years ago. The only time I really heard people swear in public was when they were gambling in Vegas, as in "Oh, God! Help me now!" or when someone was describing their recent experience hiring a company to do their website. Some people paid $25,000 for a website that turned out to be a graphic brochure. Today, you can find companies that will do a website for under $500 that includes twenty or more pages, e-mails, hosting, URL registrations, blogs, a shopping cart, and other custom features. They do it in WordPress and with a little practice, you can go into the edit mode and change pictures, text, and offerings in the shopping cart. My website was done for under $500, and it's fully functional. Once you get a website, you can splash it on your e-mail signature, your business cards, and anything and everything that people see. It is your portal to the world. When you are picking a name for your company or website, it's smart to tell them what you do in the name. While something like "Vistronical" might be a unique name, what the heck is it? When people want a speaker, especially when they want a free speaker, Free Speakers Group is a fairly easy thing to find. No one wonders what we sell. You get to see all of our speakers on the landing page, and with just one click, you can find each speaker's bio, introduction, and flyer. One page, not five or six. If it can't be said on one page with lots of white space, no one will stick around long enough to get what you have. *The fewer clicks the better!*

Less text and more pictures are ideal. We once hired a web designer for $4,000 a month, and her idea of a great page was run-on text. You'd better have lots of pictures and very little text if you want people to stay on your site. My page has two giant cartoons on it. Why? Because the message of *Fishing for Leads* is simple: walk into a room full of people you've never met, and walk out with customers! It's not rocket science—it's awareness and preparation. Later, when your business is bigger and you have cash flow, you can pay for SEO (search engine optimization), visit captures, and all kinds of stuff that you don't need to get the boat in the water. I've got a buddy in Jersey that spends $1 million a year on Google AdWords. That's his SEO. But he didn't do that when he started. He paid over $30,000 to buy a web name . . . but he didn't do that when he started. A perfect website just might earn you nothing. A clear, fully functioning website you paid less than $500 for and took less than a week to launch just might earn you a ton of money.

Now you need to build a small platoon of people who will market with you. You don't need an army, just a platoon. These people will come to you from just a few sources:

1. Past relationships, businesses, organizations, etc. The first thing I did was make a short list by going on my e-mail Outlook and, in the address bar, hitting A. All the people I have ever e-mailed that start with *A* appear in a drop-down menu. I entered the ones I thought might be willing to send twenty or more of my flyers on an Excel spreadsheet and then went on to *B*.
2. Then I went to my Facebook *friends* list, which is relatively small compared to most. I have fewer than a thousand friends. But in that group are people who would copy and paste a post I created as a post to their group. Not many will do that, but

maybe 10 percent? Some of the people in my Facebook group have over five thousand friends in their group. Just because they post doesn't mean it goes to all five thousand.

3. From the Facebook group, there are probably a few that you know who have large organizations, either MLM or a direct-sales customer list. You might want to make them an offer that if they do a direct e-mail of your flyer to their entire group, you will split profits with them (60 percent to you, 40 percent to them). To do this, you need a method of tracking where the lead came from.

4. Google what business you are in. Like I might Google *sales training* and see what comes up. If I find that some of the sites have really good e-books that complement mine, I might make them a reciprocal offer where I can offer their book as a free gift with my book, and they can offer my e-book as a bonus gift when people buy their book. They can have an affiliate listing on your site or not—you can do this kind of deal even if you don't have an "Our Friends" listing on your site.

5. Go on Amazon.com and see who has a business similar to yours. If they have electronic versions of their book, do the same thing with them—offer a reciprocal agreement. When I was marketing my book *The Cancer Conundrum*, I e-mailed another person who had written a similar book, and he gladly made the book *Hope, Medicine, and Healing* available to me as an e-book and vice versa.

6. Search for a gimmick. For this book, I found a tiny little fishing game. You've seen them, where little fish go around and around and the object of the game is to hook them. If you go to Alibaba.com on Google, I guarantee the Chinese are making them for

practically nothing, but you've got to buy a ton of them and wait two months. For the cancer book, I found a tiny little Reset button like Staples's Easy button. I was able to order them at a reasonable cost. Any kind of giveaway you can do at meetings to make your deal irresistible is a good investment. Ask yourself, how can I illustrate the core message of my book with an object? Can I find them? Can I get them made?

7. Don't forget your smart phone contacts. Page through this list and ask yourself who on this list would be willing to help you promote your business? How big is their contact list? Should you make them a partner as far as income split? My guess is, you have at least two hundred or more names in there and 10 percent will give you twenty people who can spread the word for you.

8. When the day comes that my book(s) hit the best-seller list, I'm going to throw a huge party at a local eatery. Everyone likes free drinks and eats and if you offer books for sale and sign them; you might be surprised that the food and drinks really didn't cost you anything. In the '80s I wrote a comedy book and held a reception at the Wild Flower in Boca Raton. The Boca News and WSBR radio covered the event because I had influence (friends) at both places. We had over two hundred guests show up, and I sold a ton of books. In the age of the Internet, *who you know* really is the key issue.

9. Have you kept in touch with any college friends? High school? Watch this—I moved right after junior high from Roseville, Michigan, to Detroit for high school. But my time at Guest Junior High in Roseville was some of the best years of my entire life. I had lots of close friends, Motown was in its heyday, and

we had lots of dances and wore really cool greaser clothes. It was a blast. Well, about three years ago, I contacted a few of those people via Facebook and other school links. A buddy of mine, Paul Young, organized a Guest reunion, and over fifty of us showed up. A couple of ladies looked just like they did forty-eight years ago, but most of us guys did not. I had to fly from San Diego to Detroit to attend but it was worth it. Some of those friends from way back in the '60s have been business affiliates of mine. Again, who do you know?
10. Do you have a church, temple, or mosque directory? Could you offer to donate a percentage of all your sales to a certain charity or church work? Would the pastor set up a table after church for you to present your product or service if the church could benefit? You might be surprised.

Fire Hosing on Facebook and Twitter

This one makes my stomach drop two feet. Someone joins a new MLM, and they post almost daily about this wonderful new company with the world's most lucrative compensation plan and patent-pending products that make you twenty years younger or your money back. And they do it day after day after day, until you unsubscribe them.

Want a more subtle approach? Ask one of your affiliates to send you a post that asks what you're up to lately. In a non-sales way, you can promote what you are doing. People love eavesdropping. For example,

Friend: *So, Rick, haven't really heard from you in forever. Still in San Diego? Still doing . . . what?*

Rick: *Yeah, still here in San Diego, but I've written a new book. Funnier than the last one—launches in three weeks. Send me your e-mail and I'll send you a free chapter. Other than that, chasing the grandkids around the yard, starving the dog, country-dancing on Friday night—the usual. What's new by you?*

Get the drift? If you read my post, you'd know I've got a new product, it's funny, and you can get a free sample. If you have a large following, you just might get a few hundred e-mails.

For Twitter, don't tweet the obvious sales come-on, like,

Headed to a meeting to hear about our new sensational superfood drink. I started drinking it a week ago and haven't slept since . . .

Might this work better?

Was up half the night editing my new comedy book. Dragging today. Still I nailed a few new gags. I need coffee! Can't wait till the launch is here.

What do they know? You have a new book, it's funny, and there's some kind of launch planned. If they think you are a funny guy, they will contact you for details. *Less is more!*

Even with this more subtle approach, if you overuse it, it will kill it. How about once every few weeks? You can give updates, like,

On my way to do a radio interview on the new book—hope this lady is kind. I got filleted on the last one . . .

or

Hey, some good news, book sales finally hit the Barnes and Noble best-seller list. Meet me at Hooleys this Friday after work to celebrate!

If you do this one you'd better be prepared to buy some drinks. My whole point here is that the less you say, the better. Make them wonder exactly what's going on and how can they get in on it.

If someone does a post on Facebook that they only need one hundred more people to get their five thousand names, then this is someone you want to talk to about doing some sort of reciprocal program. Page 1 of any Google search for the kind of products or service you have will probably have a huge customer list. These are your business associates, not just competitors.

Nearly all of the former or current relationships you have had or have are an untapped source for more business. But until you make it easy to buy, it won't work.

Make it Easy to Buy from You

Authors who want to solicit an endorsement for their book or project should make it easy to do. When I do a new book, I e-mail a copy of the manuscript to the person from whom I'm seeking an endorsement and a sample of what I'd like them to say—yep, I wrote the endorsements on my books, but I know them and I know what they'd say. All they need to do is approve my version in writing or if they prefer, write their own version and we are off to the races.

When I was in the vitamin business and was recruiting distributors, I'd do a presentation at their home and then have a typed-up "Going into Business" order form already filled out. All they had to do was sign it and we were done. How easy is it to do business with you? How many clicks on your website does it take to buy something?

The days of the lonesome cowboy are gone. The image of the independent person might work in pulp paperback books, but it no longer works in today's business. You need a platoon to market your idea, service, or product. You can't go at it alone. You can't do it without a website. "Fishing with Nets" now loops the whole planet in with the advent of the Internet. All these tools are yours to use.

Let's recap to reassure you that effective prospecting is not that difficult if you do it consistently.

1. "Find Five Good Fishing Holes"—visit them weekly.
2. "Change Your Bait"—one hook won't get everyone
3. "Sharpen Your Hook"—develop a few one-sentence commercials
4. "Fishing with Purpose: Your Mission Statement"
5. "Finding Hungry Fish"—getting them to ask you what you do
6. "Fishing with Nets"
   The Importance of Public Speaking
   Using the Internet and Social Media
7. "Weigh Your Catch: The Qualification Process"

Pop Quiz #5

1. What are the four basic parts of the sales process?
   _____
   _____
   _____
   _____

2. The greatest qualifier is _____

3. In order to use social media, what four things do you need to develop?
   _____
   _____
   _____
   _____

4. To develop a platoon to help you market your product, what ten things do you need to focus on?

5. Define "fire hosing."

6. Define "making yourself easy to buy from."

Porky and Daffy Graduate

I never finished the story about my episode of stuttering. After years of meeting with the school-sponsored therapist, the day came when my ninth-grade English teacher entered me into several speech contests. The first contest was for the Optimists Club. It had to be an original story based on an assigned topic. I got about halfway through and drew a blank. Totally forgot. The second contest was a dramatic reading of *Charlotte's Web*, by E.B. White.

I won at the local level, the regional level, and was at the state finals in Lansing, Michigan. There I was, facing a whole row of judges with marking pens. I got to the last line of my reading where Wilbur the pig says to Charlotte the spider, "Oh, I think you're beautiful!"

With all the drama I could muster I headed into that last line, but I feared the *B* in *beautiful* because a *B* is plosive and, as such, can cause a stutterer to "lock."

"'Oh,' said Wilbur," I said, "'I think you're bu-bu-bu-beautiful...'"

Didn't win. Placed second. But my speech therapist congratulated me when I returned and asked if I'd still like to come in and work on my math and science a little so that I could get out of high school before I hit forty.

I had graduated. Years later, when I'm signing books and getting rewarding ovations, I think back to those days, and though I'm glad they are behind me, it makes today so much better.

Do whatever you need to do, learn whatever you need to learn to be able to do these short twenty-minute free speeches, and prospect with nets instead of a hook. The interested ones will log on to your free webinar, and the serious ones will come to your events. Those who go forward with you as a coach will be the mainstream of your company.

Learning to prospect is the cornerstone of any salesperson's building. Without it, you will be at the mercy of working with anyone because you simply don't know how to replace anyone.

Don't forget to log on to http://www.freespeakersgroup.com for more information on prospecting or professional speaking. Log on to the webinar and come to the events. You and I just might wind up working together.

Hey, it could happen!

www.ingramcontent.com/pod-product-compliance
Lightning Source LLC
Chambersburg PA
CBHW030902180526
45163CB00004B/1676